RANJOT SINGH CHAHAL

# 5 Rules for Making life Simple

*Living with Purpose and Ease*

Rana Books

*First published by Rana Books (UK,INDIA) 2023*



*First edition*

*ISBN: 978-81-19786-93-0*

# Contents

V Rule 5: Foster Meaningful Connections

# I

# Rule 1: Declutter Your Physical Space

*Clear your surroundings, clear your mind. Decluttering your physical space paves the way for a clutter-free life.*

# Chapter 1: Assessing Your Belongings

Introduction:

When it comes to managing your belongings it's important to have a clear understanding of what you own and how they contribute to your life. Assessing your belongings can help you make informed decisions about what to keep what to let go of and how to organize and maintain your possessions. In this chapter we will explore the process of assessing your belongings in a detailed and practical manner. We will discuss why it's necessary different assessment techniques and provide examples to help you apply these techniques in your own life.

Understanding the Importance of Assessing Your Belongings:

1. Identifying valuable items:

Assessing your belongings enables you to identify items of value that you may not be aware of. These could include valuable antiques collectibles or even sentimental items that hold emotional value. By knowing what you have you can ensure these items are properly cared for and protected.

Example: Let's say you're going through your grandmother's old attic and come across a dusty box. Upon assessing its contents you discover a collection of rare baseball cards that are worth a significant amount of money. Without assessing your belongings you may have overlooked these valuable assets.

2. Saving space:
One of the benefits of assessing your belongings is the ability to identify items that are taking up unnecessary space. By decluttering and letting go of items you no longer need or use you can create a more organized and spacious living environment.

Example: Imagine you assess your wardrobe and find that you have several pairs of jeans that no longer fit or are outdated. By letting go of these items you can free up space in your closet for new clothes or other essential items.

3. Simplifying your life:
Assessing your belongings allows you to simplify your life by focusing on what truly matters and reducing unnecessary clutter. It helps you distinguish between items that bring you joy and those that are just adding to your mental and physical burden.

Example: You assess your book collection and realize that over time you have accumulated many books that you no longer have an interest in or plan to read. By decluttering and passing them on to someone else you simplify your bookshelf and create more mental clarity.

Techniques for Assessing Your Belongings:

1. Categorizing:

Start by categorizing your belongings into groups such as clothing books electronics kitchenware etc. This approach allows you to tackle one category at a time making the assessment process more manageable.

Example: Begin by assessing all your clothing items. Separate them into categories like tops bottoms outerwear and accessories. This will help you visualize the amount of each item you have and make informed decisions about what to keep and what to let go of.

2. Evaluating usefulness:
Evaluate each item's usefulness based on how frequently you use it and its practicality in your everyday life. Ask yourself if the item serves a purpose or if it brings you joy.

Example: Consider your kitchenware. Assess each item and determine whether you use it regularly or if it's been sitting idle for months. If you find yourself rarely using a specialty kitchen gadget it may be a good idea to let it go and free up space in your kitchen.

3. Sentimental value:
Take into account sentimental items that may not have practical use but hold emotional value. These items may include family heirlooms photographs or personalized gifts.

Example: Assess a box of old photographs. While these may not serve a practical purpose they hold sentimental value and contribute to your personal history. Decide whether you want to digitize them or display them in a photo album to preserve the memories they represent.

4. Prioritizing space:
Consider the space available in your living environment and prioritize items accordingly. This technique helps prevent overcrowding and promotes better organization.

Example: Assess your living room and review the furniture arrangement. Determine if any large or bulky items are occupying unnecessary space. By evaluating the room layout you can make adjustments and create a more spacious and functional area.

5. Assessing digital possessions:
In today's digital world assessing your digital possessions is equally important. These possessions include files on your computer emails social media accounts and online subscriptions.

Example: Assess your computer files and delete any duplicate or unnecessary documents. Organize the remaining files into folders for easy access. Review your online subscriptions and unsubscribe from any services you no longer use or need.

Conclusion:

Assessing your belongings is a crucial step in managing your possessions effectively. It helps you identify valuable items saves space simplifies your life and promotes better organization. By using techniques like categorizing evaluating usefulness considering sentimental value prioritizing space and assessing digital possessions you can apply a systematic approach to the assessment process. Remember that the goal is to create a living space that is functional clutter-free and reflects what truly matters to you. So start assessing your belongings today and enjoy the benefits of a more organized and balanced lifestyle.

# Chapter 2: Organizing Your Home

Introduction:

Organizing your home is an essential step towards creating a space that is functional efficient and aesthetically pleasing. A well-organized home not only saves time and reduces stress but also contributes to a comfortable and inviting living environment. In this chapter we will explore various techniques and strategies to help you organize your home effectively. From decluttering and sorting to creating storage solutions we will delve into the details of each step and provide practical examples to assist you in achieving an organized and harmonious living space.

## Section 1: Decluttering

### 1.1 Understanding the importance of decluttering:

Decluttering is the process of removing unnecessary and unused items from your home. It is the foundation of organizing as it helps create more space reduce visual clutter and simplify your living environment. Decluttering is not only about getting rid of physical possessions but also about evaluating their usefulness and impact on your daily life.

1.2 Sorting and categorizing:

When decluttering it is crucial to sort items into different categories based on their purpose condition and significance. This sorting process helps you determine which items to keep donate sell or discard. Some common categories include essentials sentimental items seasonal items and items for donation or disposal.

Example:

Let's imagine you are decluttering your wardrobe. Start by sorting clothes into categories like tops bottoms dresses outerwear and accessories. Then further categorize them based on seasons or occasions. This will help you identify duplicates outdated items or pieces that no longer fit making it easier to decide what to keep and what to let go.

1.3 Letting go of unnecessary items:

One of the most challenging aspects of decluttering is letting go of items that no longer serve a purpose or hold sentimental value. It is essential to be honest with yourself and evaluate whether the item brings you joy adds value to your life or aligns with your current lifestyle.

Example:

Consider a collection of old magazines that you have kept for years. Evaluate if you truly read them or if they are simply taking up space. If you rarely refer to them or can access the content online it might be time to let go and free up valuable storage space.

1.4 Donating selling or discarding items:

Once you have sorted through your belongings and identified what to let go it's time to take action. You can donate useful items to charities or individuals in need sell valuable items through online platforms or garage sales or dispose of unusable or broken items responsibly.

Example:
If you have gently used clothing that no longer fits or suits your style consider donating it to a local shelter or thrift store. This way you not only declutter your space but also contribute to a good cause and help someone in need.

Section 2: Storage Solutions

2.1 Assessing storage needs:
Every home has different storage needs based on its layout size and the items to be stored. It is essential to assess your storage requirements to create an effective organization system that maximizes space and accessibility.

Example:
A small apartment might require creative storage solutions such as using vertical space with wall-mounted shelves or utilizing under-bed storage containers. On the other hand a larger home might benefit from built-in cabinets or custom-designed closet organizers.

2.2 Utilizing vertical space:
Vertical space often overlooked provides valuable storage opportunities. By utilizing walls doors and high shelves you can free up floor space and store frequently used or decorative

items.

Example:

Install hooks on the back of doors to hold coats bags or towels. Use floating shelves to display books or decorative items. Install wall-mounted racks in the kitchen to store pots pans and utensils making them easily accessible while keeping the countertops clutter-free.

2.3 Maximizing closet space:

Closets are essential storage areas that require proper organization to optimize their functionality. Utilizing closet space efficiently involves using hangers shelves dividers and storage bins to categorize and arrange clothing shoes accessories and other personal belongings.

Example:

Use cascading hangers to maximize the hanging space for clothing like skirts pants and blouses. Invest in shoe organizers that can be hung on the back of the closet door or placed on shelves. Use drawer dividers to separate socks underwear and other small items.

2.4 Creative storage solutions:

In addition to traditional storage options there are numerous creative solutions available to maximize space in unique ways. These solutions can be customized based on individual needs and preferences.

Example:

Consider using ottomans or benches with hidden storage

compartments in the living room. Install hooks or pegboards in the garage to hang tools and equipment. Use transparent bins or labeled baskets in the pantry to easily identify and access food items.

Section 3: Maintenance and Upkeep

3.1 Regular cleaning and decluttering routines:

To maintain an organized home it is essential to establish regular cleaning and decluttering routines. Consistently dedicating time to these tasks prevents the accumulation of unnecessary items and keeps your space tidy and functional.

Example:

Set a regular schedule to declutter and clean specific areas of your home. For instance designate every Sunday afternoon for decluttering a different room or tackling a specific category such as books or kitchen utensils. Also establish a daily routine of tidying up and returning items to their designated places.

3.2 Reviewing and revising organization systems:

Over time your needs and preferences may change requiring adjustments to your organization systems. It is important to periodically review and revise your storage solutions to ensure they continue to meet your evolving needs.

Example:

As your children grow their storage requirements may change. Take the time to review and reorganize their bedrooms to accommodate their evolving interests and activities. Similarly if you acquire new belongings or hobbies reassess your existing storage solutions to make room for these additions.

Conclusion:

Organizing your home is a continuous process that requires time effort and thoughtful consideration. By following the decluttering techniques utilizing suitable storage solutions and incorporating regular maintenance routines you can create a well-organized and harmonious living environment. Remember that the goal is not to have a perfectly organized space but rather to create a functional and enjoyable home that reflects your lifestyle and brings you comfort and peace of mind.

# Chapter 3: Simplifying Your Wardrobe

Introduction:

In today's fast-paced world simplicity has become a highly sought-after lifestyle choice. One area where simplicity can be embraced is in our wardrobes. Simplifying your wardrobe can bring numerous benefits including saving time reducing decision fatigue and promoting a more sustainable lifestyle. In this chapter we will delve deeply into the art of simplifying your wardrobe providing practical tips and techniques along with relevant examples to guide you on your journey towards a more streamlined closet.

1. Assessing Your Current Wardrobe:

Before embarking on the journey of simplifying your wardrobe it is essential to assess your current clothing collection. Begin by taking inventory of all the items in your closet categorizing them based on different criteria such as style color and seasonality. This exercise will help you visualize the extent of your wardrobe and identify areas that need attention.

Example:

Sara a working professional has accumulated a vast collection of clothes over the years. During her wardrobe assessment she discovers that she owns multiple items that are similar in style and color leading to a lack of variety in her daily outfits. This realization prompts her to simplify her wardrobe and create a more cohesive and functional collection.

2. Define Your Personal Style:

Understanding your personal style is crucial when simplifying your wardrobe. By defining your style preferences you can focus on curating a collection of clothes that truly represents who you are and what you feel comfortable wearing. Consider your lifestyle body shape and color preferences to determine the clothing items that align with your personal style.

Example:

John a young entrepreneur enjoys a more casual and minimalistic style. He prefers neutral colors and streamlined silhouettes. By defining his personal style he can eliminate clothing items that don't fit his preference and focus on building a functional wardrobe that reflects his minimalist aesthetic.

3. Pare Down Your Wardrobe:

Once you have identified your personal style it's time to pare down your existing wardrobe. This involves decluttering and removing items that no longer serve you or align with your style preferences. Take a thoughtful approach and consider the following factors when deciding which items to keep or discard: fit condition versatility and sentimental value.

Example:

Maria a stay-at-home mother realizes that she has many clothing items that no longer fit her post-pregnancy body. She decides to let go of these items and only keep those that make her feel confident and comfortable. By paring down her wardrobe Maria can create a more streamlined and functional closet that suits her current lifestyle.

4. Build a Capsule Wardrobe:

A capsule wardrobe is a curated collection of versatile high-quality items that can be mixed and matched to create a variety of outfits. Building a capsule wardrobe can simplify your clothing choices and reduce clutter. Start by selecting a set number of core pieces such as tops bottoms dresses and outerwear that can be easily combined. Additionally consider including essential accessories to complete your looks.

Example:

Lisa a busy professional decides to build a capsule wardrobe for her work wardrobe. She selects a few classic blouses tailored trousers a versatile blazer and a few staple dresses. By focusing on high-quality and versatile pieces Lisa can effortlessly create professional and put-together outfits for her workweek while reducing decision fatigue.

5. Embrace Minimalism:

Minimalism is a lifestyle philosophy that advocates for reducing excess and embracing simplicity. When applied to your wardrobe minimalism promotes owning fewer items of higher quality prioritizing versatility and durability. Embracing minimalism in your wardrobe can help you make mindful purchases reduce waste and create a more sustainable lifestyle.

Example:

James a college student adopts a minimalist approach to his wardrobe. Instead of buying multiple cheaply made clothes that quickly wear out he invests in a few high-quality pieces that he can mix and match. By embracing minimalism James not only reduces his environmental footprint but also saves money in the long run.

6. Maintain a Functional Wardrobe:

Simplifying your wardrobe isn't a one-time event; it requires ongoing maintenance. It's important to regularly assess your wardrobe declutter unused items and ensure that your collection remains functional. Additionally adopt conscious shopping habits to avoid unnecessary purchases and keep your wardrobe clutter-free.

Example:

Rachel a fashion enthusiast establishes a monthly ritual of reviewing her wardrobe and decluttering any items she no longer enjoys wearing. She also refrains from impulse buying and carefully considers each purchase ensuring it aligns with her personal style and fills a gap in her collection. By maintaining a functional wardrobe Rachel can sustain the simplicity she has worked hard to achieve.

Conclusion:

Simplifying your wardrobe is a journey that requires thoughtfulness intentionality and perseverance. By assessing your current collection defining your personal style paring down your wardrobe building a capsule wardrobe embracing minimalism and maintaining functionality you can create a wardrobe that is not only simpler but also more efficient and sustainable.

Remember simplicity in your wardrobe can extend beyond aesthetics—it can positively impact your mindset productivity and overall well-being. So take this opportunity to simplify your wardrobe and embrace the many benefits that come with it.

II

# Rule 2: Simplify Your Schedule

*Streamline your schedule, simplify your life. Following Rule 2 leads to a more balanced and stress-free existence.*

# Chapter 4: Identifying Priorities

Introduction:

Identifying priorities is a crucial skill that helps individuals and organizations effectively allocate their time attention and resources. Priorities help to sort tasks goals and responsibilities in order of importance which enables individuals to focus their efforts on the most critical areas. This chapter will explore the concept of identifying priorities why it is important and provide examples and strategies for effectively identifying priorities.

Understanding Priorities:

Priorities are the tasks activities or goals that hold the highest level of importance and deserve immediate attention. They help individuals and organizations make decisions regarding resource allocation time management and goal setting. Identifying priorities requires a comprehensive understanding of the goals objectives and overall purpose of an individual or organization.

Importance of Identifying Priorities:

Identifying priorities is essential for several reasons. Firstly it helps individuals and organizations stay focused on their primary objectives preventing them from getting overwhelmed by a multitude of tasks. By allocating time and resources to the most important tasks individuals can achieve their goals more efficiently and effectively.

Secondly identifying priorities allows individuals and organizations to make informed decisions. When faced with multiple choices understanding priorities helps in determining which options align with the overarching goals. It ensures that decisions are aligned with long-term objectives rather than being based on immediate gratification or short-term gains.

Lastly identifying priorities helps individuals and organizations manage limited resources. By understanding what deserves the most attention time and resources efficient allocation can be made. This prevents wasting resources on low-priority tasks and maximizes the impact of available resources on the important areas.

Examples of Identifying Priorities:

1. Personal Priorities:

a) Health: One might prioritize regular exercise a balanced diet and sufficient sleep to maintain good physical and mental health.

b) Career: Prioritizing professional development skill enhancement and achieving career milestones could be important.

c) Relationships: Prioritizing spending quality time with family and friends nurturing meaningful connections and building a support system.

d) Personal Growth: Allocating time for personal hobbies learning new skills and pursuing self-improvement activities.

2. Work Priorities:

a) Deadlines: Identifying and prioritizing tasks based on their urgency and importance ensures that deadlines are met effectively.

b) Client Satisfaction: Prioritizing tasks that directly impact client satisfaction and relationships such as delivering high-quality work or providing exceptional customer service.

c) Revenue Generation: Identifying tasks that contribute directly to revenue generation such as sales calls or marketing campaigns as top priorities.

d) Leadership: Prioritizing tasks that support leadership responsibilities such as team management decision-making and strategic planning.

Strategies for Identifying Priorities:

1. Define Goals and Objectives: Understanding the desired outcomes and long-term objectives helps in identifying the necessary priorities. Clearly define what needs to be achieved and align tasks accordingly.

2. Assess Importance and Urgency: Categorize tasks based on their importance and urgency. The Eisenhower Matrix is a useful tool that helps classify tasks into four categories: important and urgent important but not urgent urgent but not important and not urgent and not important. Prioritize tasks based on this assessment.

3. Consider Impact and Alignment: Identify tasks that have a substantial impact on overall goals and objectives. Evaluate whether tasks align with the core purpose and values and

prioritize accordingly.

4. Time Management Techniques: Utilize time management techniques such as Pomodoro Technique or time blocking to prioritize tasks and allocate dedicated time for high-priority activities.

5. Seek Input and Collaboration: Engage with stakeholders colleagues or mentors to gain different perspectives and insights. This can help in refining priorities identifying blind spots and aligning priorities with broader organizational goals.

6. Regularly Review and Evaluate: Priorities may change over time due to shifting circumstances or evolving objectives. Regularly reviewing and evaluating priorities ensures ongoing alignment and effectiveness.

7. Learn to Say No: Recognize that not all tasks and requests are equally important. Learning to say no to low-priority tasks that do not align with goals can help in managing time and resources efficiently.

Conclusion:

Identifying priorities is a foundational skill for effective time management resource allocation and goal achievement. It helps individuals and organizations focus on the most crucial tasks make informed decisions and optimize resource utilization. By understanding personal and work priorities defining goals and utilizing strategies for prioritization individuals can enhance their productivity achieve better outcomes and lead more balanced lives.

# Chapter 5: Time Management Strategies

Introduction:

Time is a precious resource and effective time management is crucial for success in any aspect of life. Whether you're a student professional or just trying to balance various responsibilities the ability to manage your time efficiently can significantly impact productivity reduce stress and improve overall satisfaction. In this chapter we will explore various time management strategies and techniques that can help you become more organized prioritize tasks and make the most of your valuable time.

1. Prioritize and Set Goals:

One of the foundational principles of time management is setting priorities and defining clear goals. By identifying what is most important you can allocate your time and energy accordingly. Here are a few techniques to aid in prioritization:

a) Eisenhower Matrix: Developed by former U.S. President Dwight D. Eisenhower this matrix categorizes tasks into four quadrants based on their urgency and importance. The quadrants are:

- Important and Urgent: Tasks requiring immediate attention.
- Important but Not Urgent: Long-term goals or tasks that

don't have immediate deadlines.

- Urgent but Not Important: Tasks that can be delegated or eliminated.
- Not Urgent and Not Important: Time-wasting activities that should be minimized.

b) SMART Goals: Create goals that are Specific Measurable Achievable Relevant and Time-bound. This approach helps to clarify objectives and provides a framework for progress monitoring.

For example suppose you're a student with multiple assignments due. By using the Eisenhower Matrix you can identify which assignments are urgent and important allowing you to focus on those first. Setting SMART goals would involve breaking down each assignment into smaller tasks with specific deadlines.

2. Plan and Schedule:

Planning plays a crucial role in effective time management. Taking the time to create a well-thought-out schedule can help you stay organized and ensure that you allocate sufficient time for each task. Here are a couple of planning and scheduling strategies:

a) To-Do Lists: Write down all the tasks you need to accomplish and organize them according to priority. Crossing items off your list can provide a sense of accomplishment and motivate you to tackle more tasks.

b) Time Blocking: Allocate specific time blocks for different activities throughout the day. This technique helps you stay focused by dedicating designated time slots to specific tasks. For example you may allocate two hours for studying in the morning and another two hours for a creative project in the afternoon.

3. Eliminate Time Wasters:

Time wasters can be productivity killers and hinder your ability to manage time effectively. Here are a few common time wasters and strategies to overcome them:

a) Procrastination: Waiting until the last minute to start a task can lead to stress and reduced quality of work. Overcoming procrastination involves breaking tasks into smaller manageable parts and establishing deadlines for each part.

b) Distractions: In today's digital age distractions come in various forms such as social media emails and notifications. Minimize distractions by using focus apps or turning off notifications during dedicated work periods.

c) Multitasking: Contrary to popular belief multitasking can actually decrease productivity. Instead focus on one task at a time complete it and then move on to the next.

4. Delegate and Outsource:

Recognizing when tasks can be delegated or outsourced is a crucial skill for effective time management. Delegation involves assigning tasks to others who can complete them efficiently while outsourcing involves hiring external professionals or services. Here are a few scenarios where delegation or outsourcing can be beneficial:

a) Work-related tasks: If you find yourself overwhelmed with work consider delegating certain responsibilities to colleagues who have the necessary skills and knowledge.

b) Personal tasks: Hiring someone to clean your house mow your lawn or run errands can free up valuable time for more important activities.

c) Virtual Assistants: Virtual assistants can handle administrative tasks scheduling research and other time-consuming activities allowing you to focus on high-priority tasks.

5. Practice Time Batching:

Time batching involves grouping similar tasks together to increase efficiency. By reducing the context switching between different types of tasks you can minimize wasted time and improve productivity. Here are some examples of time batching:

a) Email Management: Instead of checking emails throughout the day allocate specific time blocks dedicated solely to reading and responding to emails.

b) Meetings and Collaboration: Set specific times for meetings or collaborative work to avoid interruptions in individual work.

c) Creative Work: If you have a project that requires deep focus and creativity allocate a dedicated time block where you can fully immerse yourself in the task.

6. Breaks and Rest:

While it may seem counterintuitive taking regular breaks can enhance productivity and prevent burnout. Here's how breaks can contribute to effective time management:

a) Pomodoro Technique: This technique involves working in focused 25-minute intervals followed by a short five-minute break. After completing four Pomodoros take a longer break of around 15-30 minutes. This helps maintain concentration and prevents mental fatigue.

b) Exercise and Meditation: Engaging in physical exercise or mindfulness practices like meditation can enhance focus reduce stress and increase overall productivity.

7. Learn to Say No:

One of the essential skills in time management is the ability to say no to tasks or commitments that don't align with your priorities or overload your schedule. Here are some strategies for saying no effectively:

a) Assess Priorities: When faced with additional tasks consider whether they align with your goals and if they can be accommodated within your current schedule. If they don't politely decline.

b) Provide Alternatives: If you can't take on a task but understand its importance offer alternative solutions such as suggesting another person who may be able to help.

c) Set Boundaries: Clearly communicate your availability and limitations to avoid overcommitment.

Conclusion:

Effective time management is a skill that can be developed and honed through practice and implementation of various strategies and techniques. By prioritizing tasks planning eliminating time wasters delegating when necessary practicing time batching taking breaks and learning to say no you can optimize your use of time enhance productivity and achieve a better work-life balance. Experiment with different strategies adapt them to your unique circumstances and find a time management approach that works best for you. Remember time management is not about doing more; it's about doing what matters most.

# Chapter 6: Setting Boundaries

Introduction:

Setting boundaries is an important aspect of maintaining healthy relationships maintaining personal well-being and ensuring a balanced and fulfilling life. Boundaries can be seen as the rules or limits we establish for ourselves and communicate to others regarding what we find acceptable and what we do not. They help create clarity and define personal space emotional needs and expectations in different relationships and contexts. In this chapter we will explore the significance of setting boundaries the types of boundaries and strategies for establishing and maintaining them effectively.

The Significance of Setting Boundaries:

Setting boundaries is crucial for several reasons. Firstly they promote self-respect and self-care. When we establish boundaries we acknowledge our own needs priorities and values and ensure that our well-being is not compromised. By saying no to what is not in alignment with our values or priorities we affirm our self-worth and demonstrate self-respect. Boundaries also help us manage our time and energy effectively preventing burnout and overwhelm.

Additionally setting clear boundaries nurtures healthy relationships. Healthy boundaries foster trust respect and open communication. When we communicate our boundaries to others we provide them with valuable information about our expectations and limits which allows for more harmonious interactions. Boundaries provide a framework that helps both parties understand and respect each other's individuality preferences and needs. This leads to more satisfying and fulfilling relationships.

Types of Boundaries:

Boundaries can be categorized into different types based on the area of life they pertain to. Here are some common types of boundaries:

1. Physical boundaries: These boundaries define our personal physical space and touch preferences. For example a physical boundary may involve specifying how close someone can stand to us or indicating our comfort level with physical affection.

Example: Emily has a physical boundary that she doesn't like people hugging her without her consent. She communicates this boundary to her friends and family and they respect her preference by asking for permission before hugging.

2. Emotional boundaries: Emotional boundaries are about protecting and expressing our emotions feelings and personal experiences. This involves asserting our emotional needs setting limits on emotional intimacy and avoiding emotional manipulation or abuse.

Example: Mark has an emotional boundary where he doesn't allow others to constantly criticize and belittle him. When he encounters this behavior he calmly expresses that it hurts him and requests a more respectful approach in the future.

3. Intellectual boundaries: Intellectual boundaries involve respecting and valuing each person's thoughts ideas and opinions without invalidation or infringement. It allows for open dialogue and encourages individuals to express themselves without fear of judgment or ridicule.

Example: Sarah has an intellectual boundary where she values constructive criticism but won't tolerate personal attacks on her ideas. When someone crosses this boundary by resorting to name-calling or insults she calmly reminds them to focus on the discussion at hand.

4. Time boundaries: Time boundaries help manage and protect our time ensuring that we allocate it to activities and people that align with our priorities and goals. This involves setting time limits creating schedules and learning to say no to activities that don't align with our priorities.

Example: Jason has a time boundary where he sets aside specific periods for focused work and avoids distractions during those times. He communicates this boundary to colleagues and family members requesting their understanding and cooperation.

5. Material boundaries: Material boundaries deal with personal belongings finances and resources. They involve establishing limits on what is shared borrowed or used by others. These

boundaries protect our material possessions and ensure fair treatment in financial transactions.

Example: Karen has a material boundary where she clearly communicates that her personal belongings are off-limits unless she gives explicit permission to borrow them. She also sets expectations around repayment when lending money to friends.

Establishing Boundaries:

Establishing boundaries can be challenging especially if we are not accustomed to doing so. However with practice and self-awareness it becomes easier. Here are some strategies to help you establish boundaries effectively:

1. Self-reflection: Understand your needs values and limits before communicating them to others. Spend time reflecting on what is important to you and consider where you may need to set boundaries to honor your well-being and priorities.

2. Clear communication: Clearly and assertively communicate your boundaries to others. Use "I" statements to express your needs and expectations avoiding blame or judgment. Be direct concise and respectful while outlining your boundaries.

3. Consistency: Consistency is key to maintaining boundaries. Ensure that you enforce your boundaries consistently and do not compromise on what you have clearly communicated. This will help others understand the importance of your boundaries and establish a pattern of respect.

4. Emotional resilience: Be prepared for potential pushback or resistance from others when you establish boundaries. People may try to test or challenge your boundaries but it's essential to stay firm and not give in to guilt or manipulation.

5. Flexibility and negotiation: While boundaries are important it's also important to recognize that relationships require flexibility and negotiation. Be open to discussing and adjusting boundaries if necessary while still considering your own well-being.

Maintaining Boundaries:

Once boundaries are established it is crucial to maintain them consistently. Here are some tips for maintaining boundaries effectively:

1. Self-awareness: Continually check in with yourself to ensure that your boundaries are still aligned with your needs and priorities. Regularly assess if any adjustments or additions are required.

2. Assertiveness: Be assertive in enforcing your boundaries. Respectfully remind others of your boundaries when they are crossed and take appropriate action if necessary. Practice saying no when something doesn't align with your boundaries.

3. Self-care: Prioritize self-care to avoid burnout or neglecting your own needs. Make time for activities that recharge you physically emotionally and mentally. When you take care of yourself you are better equipped to maintain your boundaries.

4. Seek support: Surround yourself with people who understand and respect your boundaries. Seek support from friends family or professionals who can provide guidance and encouragement as you navigate boundary-related challenges.

Conclusion:

Setting boundaries is a crucial aspect of leading a healthy fulfilling and balanced life. By establishing and maintaining boundaries we honor our needs values and priorities while nurturing healthy relationships with others. Whether it's physical emotional intellectual time or material boundaries they provide a framework for self-respect open communication and mutual understanding. With self-awareness clear communication and consistency we can effectively establish and maintain boundaries that contribute to our well-being and enhance the quality of our relationships.

# III

# Rule 3: Cultivate Mindfulness

*Discover the transformative power of staying present in every moment, enriching your life with awareness and inner peace.*

# Chapter 7: Practicing Mindful Awareness

Introduction:

In today's fast-paced world where distractions abound and stress levels are high the practice of mindful awareness offers a valuable tool for cultivating a sense of peace clarity and groundedness. Mindful awareness involves intentionally paying attention to the present moment without judgment or attachment to our thoughts feelings or external circumstances. It allows us to fully immerse ourselves in the here and now and develop a deep understanding of our inner experiences.

In this chapter we will delve deeply into the practice of mindful awareness exploring its benefits techniques and exercises. Through a variety of examples and practical applications we will elucidate the power of mindful awareness in different aspects of our lives.

1. Benefits of Mindful Awareness:

Mindful awareness has numerous benefits for our mental emotional and physical well-being. Let's take a closer look at some of the key advantages:

a) Reduced Stress and Anxiety: Mindful awareness helps us break free from the grip of stress and anxiety by bringing our attention to the present moment and promoting a sense of calmness and relaxation.

Example: Imagine you are facing a challenging and high-pressure situation at work. Instead of succumbing to stress and anxiety you can practice mindful awareness by focusing on your breath bodily sensations and thoughts. This can help shift your attention away from stressors and bring a sense of groundedness and clarity.

b) Improved Emotional Regulation: Mindful awareness allows us to observe our emotions without judgment or reaction. It helps us develop emotional intelligence and the ability to respond to our feelings in a skillful and adaptive manner.

Example: Let's say you encounter a frustrating situation that triggers anger within you. By practicing mindful awareness you can observe the arising anger notice the bodily sensations associated with it and acknowledge the emotions without getting caught up in them. This enables you to respond more effectively and constructively to the situation rather than impulsively reacting out of anger.

c) Enhanced Concentration and Focus: Mindful awareness strengthens our ability to concentrate and sustain attention. It trains our minds to resist distractions and stay fully engaged in the present moment leading to improved focus and productivity.

Example: During a meditation practice of mindful awareness

you might notice your mind wandering away from the present moment and getting caught up in thoughts or external distractions. By gently redirecting your attention back to your breath or anchor point you cultivate the ability to maintain focus and concentration which can be transferred to various tasks in your daily life.

2. Techniques for Practicing Mindful Awareness:

There are numerous techniques and exercises to cultivate mindful awareness. Let's explore a few popular ones:

a) Mindful Breathing: This technique involves focusing your attention on the natural rhythm of your breath. Notice the sensation of the breath as it enters and leaves your body without trying to control or manipulate it.

Example: Find a comfortable position either sitting or lying down. Close your eyes and bring your attention to your breath. Notice the sensation of the breath as it enters your nostrils fills your lungs and exits through your mouth. If your mind wanders gently bring it back to the breath. Practice this for a few minutes each day to develop your capacity for mindful awareness.

b) Body Scan Meditation: This technique involves systematically bringing awareness to different parts of your body starting from the top of your head and moving downward.

Example: Begin by closing your eyes and taking a few deep breaths. Direct your attention to the top of your head and notice any sensations or tension present there. Slowly move your attention downward scanning each part of your body including your face neck shoulders arms hands chest abdomen pelvis legs and feet. Observe any sensations discomfort or areas of tension without judgment. Take your time and be present with each body part.

c) Mindful Eating: This technique involves bringing awareness to the process of eating paying attention to the taste texture and sensations of the food as well as the act of chewing and swallowing.

Example: Before starting a meal take a moment to pause and bring your attention to the food in front of you. Notice the colors shapes and smells. Take a bite and savor it fully paying attention to the flavors textures and sensations in your mouth. Chew slowly and mindfully noticing the changes in taste and texture as you continue to eat. Be fully present with each bite without distractions or rushing.

3. Practical Applications of Mindful Awareness:

Mindful awareness is not limited to formal meditation practices; it can be applied to various aspects of our lives. Let's explore some practical applications:

a) Mindful Communication: Mindful awareness can enhance our communication skills by enabling us to listen attentively speak thoughtfully and respond skillfully in conversations.

Example: During a conversation with a colleague practice mindful awareness by giving your full attention to what they are saying. Listen deeply without interrupting or preparing your response in advance. Notice any judgments assumptions or emotions arising within you and aim to respond from a place of understanding and empathy.

b) Mindful Movement: Mindful awareness can be integrated into physical activities such as walking yoga or even household chores. It involves bringing attention to the sensations movements and breath associated with the activity.

Example: While walking consciously bring your attention to the sensations in your feet as they touch the ground. Notice the shifting weight the movement of your legs and the rhythm of your breath. Engage all your senses and remain fully present with each step rather than allowing your mind to wander or be preoccupied with thoughts.

c) Mindful Work: Mindful awareness can enhance our productivity and job satisfaction by cultivating focus reducing stress and promoting a sense of purpose and presence in our work.

Example: Before starting a work task take a moment to ground yourself through mindful awareness. Notice any tension or distractions in your body and mind and consciously release them. Bring your attention fully to the task at hand without getting caught up in worries about the past or future. Notice the sensations thoughts and emotions arising as you work and maintain a non-judgmental stance towards them.

Conclusion:

In conclusion the practice of mindful awareness is a powerful tool for cultivating peace clarity and resilience in our daily lives. By intentionally directing our attention to the present moment without judgment or attachment we can experience a range of benefits including reduced stress improved emotional regulation enhanced concentration and greater overall well-being.

Through techniques such as mindful breathing body scan meditation and mindful eating we can develop the skills necessary to bring mindful awareness into various aspects of our lives. Whether it's in our communication movement or work the practice of mindful awareness enables us to live more fully and authentically.

So take a moment now to pause bring your attention to your breath and experience the present moment in all its richness. Embrace the practice of mindful awareness and let it transform your life.

# Chapter 8: Staying Present in the Moment

Introduction:

In today's fast-paced world staying present in the moment has become increasingly challenging. With the constant distractions and obligations that come our way it's easy to get caught up in the past or worry about the future. However by cultivating the practice of staying present we can experience greater clarity peace and fulfillment in our lives.

In this chapter we will explore the concept of staying present in the moment its benefits and practical techniques to incorporate into our daily lives. Through examples and exercises we will delve deeper into how we can develop mindfulness and create a greater sense of presence.

1. Understanding Mindfulness:

Mindfulness is the foundation of staying present in the moment. It involves paying attention intentionally without judgment to the present moment and experiencing it fully. By cultivating mindfulness we can heighten our awareness of our thoughts emotions sensations and surroundings.

Imagine you are taking a walk in a beautiful park. Instead of getting lost in thoughts about work or your to-do list you focus on the sensations of walking the sounds of nature and the sights around you. You allow yourself to fully immerse in the present moment without judgments or distractions embracing the experience with all your senses.

2. Benefits of Staying Present:

Staying present in the moment has numerous benefits for our mental emotional and physical well-being. Let's explore some of the key advantages below:

a) Reduced stress and anxiety: When we stay present we detach ourselves from worries about the past or future alleviating stress and anxiety. By focusing on the present moment we can mitigate the negative effects of rumination and overthinking.

b) Enhanced focus and concentration: By directing our attention towards the present we improve our focus and concentration. This can lead to increased productivity improved decision-making and enhanced performance in various aspects of our lives.

c) Deeper connections and relationships: When we are fully present with others we create deeper connections and build stronger relationships. By giving our undivided attention and truly listening we can foster empathy understanding and meaningful connections.

d) Improved self-awareness: Staying present allows us to

become more aware of our thoughts emotions and patterns of behavior. This self-awareness provides valuable insights into our inner workings enabling personal growth and the ability to make conscious choices.

e) Heightened enjoyment and fulfillment: By being fully present in the moment we can savor life's experiences more deeply. We become more attuned to moments of joy beauty and gratitude enhancing our overall sense of fulfillment and well-being.

3. Techniques for Staying Present:

Now that we have explored the benefits of staying present let's dive into some practical techniques to cultivate mindfulness in our daily lives:

a) Mindful breathing: Paying attention to our breath is a powerful way to anchor ourselves in the present moment. By focusing on the sensations of inhaling and exhaling we bring our attention to the present. Try taking a few deep breaths noticing the rise and fall of your abdomen or the sensation of air entering and leaving your nostrils.

b) Body scan meditation: This technique involves scanning our body from head to toe paying attention to any sensations or areas of tension. By bringing awareness to our physical body we can reconnect with the present moment. Start by gently scanning your body noticing areas of warmth tension or relaxation.

c) Engaging the senses: Engaging our senses is a powerful way to anchor ourselves in the present. Take a moment to notice the sights sounds smells tastes and tactile sensations around you. Fully immerse yourself in these experiences appreciating the richness of the present moment.

d) Cultivating gratitude: Practicing gratitude shifts our focus from what's lacking in our lives to what's present and positive. Take a few moments each day to reflect on what you are grateful for. This exercise helps develop a greater appreciation for the present moment.

e) Mindful activities: Engaging in everyday activities mindfully can deepen our connection to the present moment. Whether it's eating a meal washing the dishes or even brushing our teeth we can bring our full attention to these activities. Notice the sensations smells and tastes involved engaging all your senses.

f) Letting go of judgments: Judgments and evaluations often pull us away from the present moment. By cultivating non-judgmental awareness we can observe our thoughts and experiences without clinging to them. Practice accepting things as they are without labeling them as good or bad.

g) Mindfulness in social interactions: In our interactions with others practice being fully present and attentive. Make eye contact listen actively and be genuinely interested. By giving your full attention you enhance the quality of your connections and build deeper relationships.

h) Daily mindfulness practice: Incorporating a regular mindfulness practice into your routine can greatly support staying present in the moment. Whether it's through meditation journaling or mindful movement dedicating time each day to strengthen your mindfulness muscles can create lasting changes.

Conclusion:

Staying present in the moment is a powerful practice that can transform our lives. By cultivating mindfulness and incorporating practical techniques we can experience reduced stress enhanced focus deeper connections and greater fulfillment. Remember being present is not about perfection or complete eradication of thoughts; it is about gentle awareness and acceptance of the present moment. With practice and patience you can develop the skill of staying present bringing more clarity joy and peace into your life. So embrace the beauty of each moment and embark on your journey towards greater presence today.

# Chapter 9: Mindful Stress Management

Introduction:

Stress is an inevitable part of life. It can arise from various sources such as work pressures relationship conflicts financial difficulties or health-related problems. While some amount of stress can be motivating and beneficial excessive and chronic stress can have detrimental effects on our mental emotional and physical well-being. Therefore it is essential to develop effective stress management techniques to maintain a healthy balance in our lives.

In recent years mindfulness-based stress reduction techniques have gained popularity as powerful tools for managing and reducing stress. Mindfulness rooted in ancient Buddhist meditation practices involves consciously paying attention to the present moment with non-judgmental awareness. By cultivating mindful awareness individuals can gain insight into their thoughts emotions and bodily sensations and develop a compassionate and accepting attitude towards themselves and their experiences. This chapter aims to explore the concept of mindful stress management and provide practical examples of how it can be integrated into our daily lives.

Understanding Stress:

Before delving into mindful stress management it is crucial to understand the nature and impact of stress. Stress is a natural response that occurs when we perceive a threat or demand that exceeds our coping abilities. It triggers a physiological response commonly known as the "fight-or-flight" response which prepares our bodies to deal with the perceived threat. While this response can be useful in short-term situations chronic activation of the stress response can have negative consequences on our health.

Chronic stress can lead to various physical and psychological symptoms including exhaustion irritability anxiety depression sleep problems and decreased immune functioning. It can also contribute to the development or exacerbation of numerous health conditions such as cardiovascular disease diabetes gastrointestinal disorders and weakened immune system.

Mindful Stress Management Techniques:

1. Mindful Breathing:

One of the fundamental techniques in mindful stress management is mindful breathing. By focusing our attention on our breath we redirect our awareness to the present moment and disengage from stress-inducing thoughts. This technique can be practiced in any situation whether it's at work home or during a stressful event.

To practice mindful breathing find a comfortable position and take a few deep breaths to relax. Then shift your attention to your breath noticing the sensation of your inhalation and exhalation. Allow your breath to flow naturally without trying to control it. If your mind wanders gently bring your attention back to your breath without judgment. Repeat this practice for a few minutes to experience a sense of calm and relaxation.

2. Body Scan Meditation:

Another powerful technique in mindful stress management is body scan meditation. This practice involves systematically directing our attention to different parts of the body observing any sensations or tensions without judgment. By cultivating awareness of the body we can release physical and mental tension promoting deep relaxation.

To practice body scan meditation find a quiet and comfortable space. Start by lying down or sitting in a relaxed position. Close your eyes and bring your attention to your body starting from the top of your head. Gradually move your attention downwards scanning each body part from head to toe. Notice any sensations or areas of tension and allow your breath to soften and release any bodily discomfort. Continue this practice for 10-15 minutes or as long as it feels comfortable.

3. Mindful Eating:

Eating mindfully is not only beneficial for our physical health but also helps us manage stress. By bringing awareness to our eating habits we can savor the flavors textures and nourishment of food promoting healthier choices and reducing emotional eating.

To practice mindful eating start by choosing a meal or snack. Before you begin eating take a moment to observe the colors shapes and smells of the food on your plate. As you start eating slow down your pace and pay attention to the taste texture and sensations that arise. Notice the urge to rush or get distracted and bring your attention back to the present moment. Chew your food thoroughly and savor each bite without judgment. By practicing mindful eating you can enhance your connection with food and improve your digestion.

4. Mindful Movement:

Engaging in mindful movement practices such as yoga tai chi or walking meditation can help reduce stress and promote a sense of calm and well-being. These practices involve combining physical movements with conscious awareness allowing us to become fully present in our bodies.

Yoga for example combines gentle postures breathwork and meditation to promote relaxation and flexibility. By mindfully attuning to our body's sensations and breath we can release tension increase our body awareness and cultivate a sense of inner peace.

Tai chi on the other hand is a graceful form of ancient Chinese martial arts that focuses on slow and deliberate movements. By syncing our breath with these flowing movements we can improve balance flexibility and mental clarity.

Walking meditation involves walking slowly and deliberately paying attention to the sensations of each step. By attuning to our walking experience we can anchor ourselves in the present moment and promote relaxation and awareness.

5. Mindful Communication:

Effective communication is essential for managing stress in relationships and workplace settings. Mindful communication involves listening and speaking with full and reducing mis andTo communication try steps Prior listening on maintaining eye and without Aim and your judgment Pause take before or. to than impuls- compassion trying to understand others' perspec-tives even if This foster reduceConclusionful offer for and-being cultivating we develop relationship allowing to with resilience and. mindful body mindful or integrating these our lives us more greater. with and remember that mindfulness is a practice that requires ongoing commitment and self-compassion.

# IV

# Rule 4: Embrace Minimalism

*Unlock the freedom and clarity that come with simplifying your life, focusing on what truly matters, and letting go of excess*

# Chapter 10: The Benefits of Minimalism

Introduction:

Minimalism is a lifestyle that emphasizes simplicity and purposeful living. It encourages individuals to prioritize what truly matters and remove unnecessary clutter both physical and mental from their lives. Adopting a minimalist approach can have numerous benefits that positively impact various aspects of one's life.

1. Reduce Stress and Overwhelm:

One major advantage of minimalism is its ability to reduce stress and overwhelm. In today's fast-paced and consumer-driven society people often find themselves surrounded by excessive possessions and commitments leading to a constant feeling of being overwhelmed. By embracing minimalism individuals intentionally simplify their lives and eliminate unnecessary distractions resulting in reduced stress levels. This intentional simplicity also helps individuals focus on what truly matters promoting a sense of peace and well-being.

For example imagine a person who owns a large number of clothes most of which they rarely wear. Their wardrobe is cluttered and disorganized making it difficult for them to find what they need. This constant struggle to locate items can lead to frustration and stress. By adopting minimalism they can declutter their wardrobe keeping only the items they love and wear regularly. This not only simplifies their morning routine but also reduces the stress associated with decision-making and clutter.

2. Financial Freedom:

Minimalism enables individuals to free themselves from consumerism and excessive material possessions which in turn can lead to enhanced financial freedom. By resisting the urge to accumulate unnecessary items individuals can save money reduce debt and live within their means. This financial flexibility allows them to prioritize experiences relationships and personal growth over material possessions.

For instance consider a couple who were once caught in the cycle of constant consumerism acquiring new gadgets furniture and clothes without much thought. However they realized that this lifestyle was not sustainable both financially and emotionally. They decided to adopt minimalism focusing on buying only what they truly needed and valued. This change in mindset allowed them to pay off debts save for meaningful experiences like travel and ultimately achieve a greater sense of financial security and freedom.

3. Enhanced Mental Clarity and Focus:

Minimalism extends beyond physical possessions and encompasses mental clutter as well. By eliminating unnecessary distractions and simplifying one's environment individuals can cultivate enhanced mental clarity and focus. This mental decluttering allows people to better prioritize their thoughts goals and actions leading to increased productivity and overall well-being.

For example imagine a student who constantly feels overwhelmed by numerous commitments including extracurricular activities part-time work and social obligations. This constant juggling of responsibilities can hinder their ability to focus on their studies and leads to increased stress levels. By embracing minimalism they can streamline their commitments and eliminate unnecessary activities allowing them to concentrate on their academic pursuits and reduce mental clutter.

4. Improved Relationships and Emotional Well-being:
Minimalism promotes meaningful connections and quality relationships. By detaching from material possessions and focusing on experiences and human connection individuals can deepen their relationships and cultivate a greater sense of emotional well-being. Minimalism encourages people to invest time and energy into the people and experiences that truly matter to them rather than pouring resources into possessions.

For instance consider a family that spends most of their time consumed by materialistic pursuits and accumulating possessions. As a result they have minimal quality time together and their relationships suffer. By adopting minimalism they can prioritize family activities spending quality time together and creating lasting memories. This shift in focus improves their relationships enhances their emotional well-being and strengthens their family bonds.

5. Environmental Sustainability:
Minimalism aligns with the principles of environmental sustainability. By consuming less and rejecting excessive consumerism individuals can reduce their carbon footprint and contribute to a more environmentally friendly lifestyle. Minimalism encourages people to question their consumption habits and make conscious choices that positively impact the planet.

For example imagine an individual who consistently buys new gadgets and electronics discarding old ones without much thought. By adopting minimalism they become more mindful of their consumption habits. Instead of constantly upgrading to the latest technology they consider the environmental impact of their actions and choose to repair or repurpose their existing devices. This shift towards mindful consumption minimizes waste and supports sustainability.

In conclusion minimalism offers numerous benefits that can positively impact different aspects of one's life. By embracing minimalism individuals can reduce stress and overwhelm achieve greater financial freedom enhance mental clarity and focus improve relationships and emotional well-being and contribute to environmental sustainability. Embracing intentional simplicity and purposeful living allows individuals to create a life that is aligned with their values and priorities leading to a more fulfilling and satisfying existence.

# Chapter 11: Letting Go of Excess

Introduction:

In today's fast-paced consumer-driven society it's easy to accumulate excess. Whether it's material possessions digital clutter or emotional baggage the burden of excess can weigh us down and hinder our ability to lead fulfilling lives. In this chapter we will delve deeply into the concept of letting go of excess exploring its various forms and providing practical strategies to help you simplify and find freedom.

1. Letting go of material possessions:

Our attachment to material possessions often leads to clutter in our homes and minds. Letting go of excess in this area involves decluttering and embracing minimalism. Start by assessing your belongings and identifying what truly brings value and joy to your life. Consider donating selling or throwing away items that no longer serve a purpose. Marie Kondo's method of decluttering popularized by her book "The Life-Changing Magic of Tidying Up encourages asking yourself if an item sparks joy. By letting go of excess material possessions you create space for what truly matters.

Example: Sarah had always been a collector of items—books

clothes gadgets. Her home was filled to the brim with things she rarely used. One day she stumbled upon the concept of minimalism and decided to embark on a journey of letting go. Sarah started by going through her book collection realizing that many books had been collecting dust for years. She sold or donated the ones she no longer needed and created a space for a cozy reading nook instead. Gradually she extended the same process to her clothes kitchenware and other possessions. As Sarah let go of excess she noticed a sense of lightness and freedom in her life.

2. Letting go of digital clutter:
In the digital age excess can manifest itself in the form of digital clutter—unused apps overflowing email inboxes and an endless stream of notifications. Letting go of digital excess involves organizing and prioritizing your digital presence. Start by decluttering your devices deleting unnecessary apps and organizing digital files and folders. Unsubscribe from newsletters and mailing lists that no longer interest you. Develop healthy digital habits such as setting boundaries for screen time and prioritizing meaningful interactions over mindless scrolling.

Example: John found himself constantly checking his phone drowning in a sea of notifications and virtual distractions. He realized that he needed to let go of his digital excess to regain control of his time and attention. John began by uninstalling apps that he rarely used and organized the remaining ones into categorized folders. He then set specific times for checking emails and turned off non-essential notifications. As a result John experienced a newfound sense of focus and clarity in his daily life.

3. Letting go of emotional baggage:

Excess can take an emotional toll on us as well. Emotional baggage can manifest as negative thoughts grudges or unresolved issues from the past. Letting go of emotional excess involves healing and finding closure. Start by acknowledging and accepting your emotions. Create a safe space for yourself to express and process these feelings whether through journaling therapy or meditation. Practice forgiveness both towards others and yourself. By releasing emotional baggage you create room for personal growth and inner peace.

Example: Lisa had gone through a difficult breakup that left her emotionally drained. She carried the baggage of resentment and heartbreak for years which affected her ability to form new relationships. One day Lisa decided it was time to let go and find closure. She sought professional help and engaged in therapy sessions to explore her emotions and develop healthy coping mechanisms. Through this process Lisa gradually released her emotional baggage allowing herself to heal and embrace new opportunities for love and happiness.

4. Letting go of excess commitments:

Excess commitments can leave us feeling overwhelmed and spread thin. Letting go of excess commitments involves setting boundaries and prioritizing what truly matters to us. Start by reviewing your commitments and identifying which ones align with your values and goals. Learn to say no graciously to new commitments that do not serve your overall well-being. Delegate tasks when possible and focus on activities that bring you joy and fulfillment. By letting go of excess commitments you can create a more balanced and meaningful life.

Example: Mark was always the go-to person for assisting others with their projects often leaving him with little time for his own pursuits. As a result he felt overwhelmed and unsatisfied. Mark decided it was time to let go of excess commitments and reclaim his time. He started by setting boundaries and politely declining new requests that didn't align with his values and priorities. He also began delegating tasks to capable colleagues allowing him to focus on meaningful projects that inspired him. Mark found that by letting go of excess commitments he regained a sense of control and regained his passion for his work.

Conclusion:

Letting go of excess is a transformative process that can free us from the shackles of accumulation and clutter in all areas of our lives. By decluttering our material possessions organizing our digital lives releasing emotional baggage and setting boundaries with excess commitments we create space for what truly matters—creating a more fulfilling and purposeful life. Letting go is an ongoing practice that requires self-reflection mindfulness and the willingness to embrace change. As you embark on this journey remember that letting go of excess is the gateway to living a life of simplicity freedom and inner peace.

# Chapter 12: Living with Intention

Introduction:

Living with intention refers to living a purposeful and meaningful life where every action and decision is guided by one's values goals and core beliefs. It is about aligning one's actions with their true desires and priorities rather than simply going through the motions or being swept away by external influences. When we live with intention we take control of our lives and create a sense of fulfillment satisfaction and joy. In this chapter we will explore the concept of living with intention its benefits and practical strategies for incorporating intentionality into various aspects of life.

Understanding Intention:

Intention can be defined as a conscious and deliberate mental state that directs our actions towards a specific goal or purpose. It involves being aware of our choices and actively shaping our lives in accordance with our values and aspirations. Living with intention means being fully present in the moment and making decisions that align with our true selves.

Benefits of Living with Intention:

1. Clarity and Purpose: Living with intention helps us gain clarity about our values goals and purpose in life. It allows us to define what truly matters to us and prioritize our actions accordingly.

2. Increased Self-Awareness: By living with intention we become more self-aware understanding our strengths weaknesses passions and values. This self-awareness helps us make conscious choices that align with who we truly are and what we want to achieve.

3. Reduced Stress and Overwhelm: When we live with intention we focus on what truly matters to us and eliminate distractions. This reduces stress and overwhelm as we are not constantly pulled in multiple directions or wasting energy on activities that do not contribute to our larger goals.

4. Enhanced Well-being: Living intentionally allows us to cultivate a greater sense of well-being and satisfaction. By aligning our actions with our values we experience a deeper sense of purpose and fulfillment in our daily lives.

Practical Strategies for Living with Intention:

1. Reflection and Self-Discovery:

Living with intention requires deep self-reflection and self-discovery. Take the time to understand your values passions and goals. Ask yourself questions such as:

- What are my core values?
- What brings me joy and fulfillment?

- What are my long-term goals and aspirations?
- What are my strengths and weaknesses?

By gaining clarity about these aspects you can start aligning your actions and decisions with your true self.

2. Setting Clear Intentions:

Once you have gained clarity about what matters most to you it is important to set clear intentions for various aspects of your life. These intentions act as guiding principles and help you stay focused on what you want to achieve. For example:

- In your career: Set intentions for the type of work you want to do the impact you want to make and the values you want to uphold.
- In your relationships: Set intentions for the kind of connections you want to have the values you want to embody in your relationships and how you want to show up for others.
- In your personal growth: Set intentions for the skills you want to develop the habits you want to cultivate and the values you want to live by.

3. Mindfulness and Presence:

Living with intention requires being fully present in the moment and mindful of your thoughts feelings and actions. Practice mindfulness by bringing your attention to the present moment and noticing any automatic or unconscious behaviors. Start observing your thoughts emotions and reactions without judgment and consciously choose your responses. This helps you make intentional decisions and avoid getting caught up in autopilot mode.

4. Prioritization and Time Management:

Living with intention involves prioritizing your time and energy on activities that align with your values and goals. Evaluate your commitments and eliminate or delegate tasks that do not contribute to your larger vision. Use effective time management techniques such as planning setting deadlines and creating to-do lists to ensure you are investing your time in activities that truly matter.

Examples of Living with Intention:

1. Career:

John is a software engineer who loves technology but feels unfulfilled in his current job. He takes the time to reflect on his values and discovers that he is passionate about sustainable living. With a clear intention to align his career with his values he starts exploring opportunities in companies that focus on renewable energy. Eventually he lands a job as a software engineer at a solar energy company where he feels a sense of purpose and alignment.

2. Health and Wellness:

Sarah wants to prioritize her health and well-being but often finds herself neglecting self-care in favor of work and other responsibilities. She reflects on her values and realizes that her health is non-negotiable. With a clear intention to live a balanced and healthy life she starts scheduling regular exercise meditation and self-care activities into her daily routine. By prioritizing her health she experiences increased energy improved mood and a greater sense of well-being.

3. Relationships:

Emma wants to cultivate deeper and more meaningful connections with her loved ones. She sets the intention to be fully present and engaged in her relationships. When spending time with her family or friends she puts away her phone actively listens and asks meaningful questions. By being intentional in her interactions Emma strengthens her relationships and creates moments of genuine connection.

4. Personal Growth:

Mark wants to become a better public speaker but feels anxious about speaking in front of large audiences. He sets the intention to overcome his fear and improve his public speaking skills. He joins a public speaking club practices regularly and seeks feedback to enhance his skills. Mark's intentional efforts pay off as his confidence grows and he becomes a skilled and confident public speaker.

Conclusion:

Living with intention is about consciously shaping our lives in alignment with our values passions and goals. By practicing self-reflection setting clear intentions and cultivating mindfulness we can create a life that is purposeful fulfilling and meaningful. Living with intention allows us to make conscious choices eliminate distractions and prioritize what truly matters to us. It is through intentional living that we can experience a greater sense of clarity well-being and fulfillment in all aspects of life.

# V

# Rule 5: Foster Meaningful Connections

*To nurture deeper relationships, create lasting bonds, and find genuine fulfillment through meaningful human interactions.*

# Chapter 13: Nurturing Relationships

Introduction:

In today's interconnected and digital world building and nurturing relationships is a crucial aspect of both personal and professional success. Strong relationships play a pivotal role in various domains including friendships families romantic partnerships and business collaborations. Nurturing relationships involves a combination of effective communication empathy trust-building and continuous effort to strengthen and maintain connection. In this chapter we will explore the importance of nurturing relationships and provide practical examples to help you enhance your relationship-building skills.

Section 1: Building Strong Foundations

1. Effective Communication:

One of the key elements in nurturing relationships is effective communication. Clear open and honest communication promotes understanding builds trust and fosters a deeper connection with others. It involves actively listening expressing oneself clearly and being responsive to the needs and emotions of the other person. For example in a friendship sharing personal experiences actively listening to each other's concerns and offering support and advice can strengthen the bond between friends.

2. Empathy:

Empathy is the ability to understand and share the feelings of another. It is an essential component of nurturing relationships as it allows individuals to connect on a deeper emotional level. When you empathize with someone you demonstrate that you care about their experiences and feelings. For instance in a romantic relationship being empathetic towards your partner's challenges and validating their emotions can create a sense of security and closeness.

3. Trust-building:

Trust is the foundation of all relationships and nurturing it is crucial for long-lasting connections. Trust is developed through consistency reliability and confidentiality. When you trust someone you believe in their honesty integrity and intentions. Building trust takes time and effort but it is worth it. In a professional setting honoring commitments maintaining confidentiality and respecting boundaries can foster trust between colleagues.

Section 2: Enhancing Relationships

1. Quality Time:

Spending quality time with loved ones is an integral part of nurturing relationships. It involves dedicating undivided attention and creating positive experiences together. For example in a family setting aside a specific time for activities such as family dinners game nights or vacations can strengthen the bond between family members.

2. Emotional Support:

Providing emotional support is essential for nurturing relationships especially during challenging times. It involves being available understanding and validating the emotions of others. For instance supporting a friend going through a difficult breakup by offering a listening ear comforting them and reminding them of their strengths can deepen the friendship.

3. Celebrating Achievements:

Acknowledging and celebrating each other's achievements can foster a supportive and positive environment in relationships. By showing genuine appreciation for the accomplishments of others you reinforce their self-esteem and create a sense of camaraderie. For example celebrating a colleague's promotion or a friend's success in a personal goal can enhance the bond between individuals.

Section 3: Conflict Resolution and Growth

1. Conflict Resolution:

No relationship is free of conflicts and learning how to navigate them is crucial for maintaining and nurturing connections. Conflict resolution involves addressing disagreements or misunderstandings in a respectful and constructive manner. Active listening expressing concerns without blame and finding a compromise are essential skills in resolving conflicts. For example in a romantic relationship discussing differences openly seeking mutually beneficial solutions and showing empathy can strengthen the bond between partners.

2. Forgiveness:

Forgiveness is a powerful tool for nurturing relationships. It involves letting go of grudges resentments and past hurts to move forward with a renewed sense of understanding and compassion. Forgiveness requires empathy understanding and the willingness to rebuild trust. For instance forgiving a friend for a mistake and giving them a second chance can strengthen their friendship.

3. Personal Growth and Development:

Nurturing relationships also involve supporting each other's personal growth and development. Encouraging and empowering loved ones to pursue their dreams learn new skills and overcome challenges can enhance their self-esteem and strengthen the bond between individuals. For example supporting a partner's career aspirations or a friend's decision to pursue higher education demonstrates investment in their personal growth.

Conclusion:

Nurturing relationships is an ongoing and enriching process that requires continuous effort and commitment. By practicing effective communication empathy trust-building and conflict resolution individuals can build and strengthen their connections with others. Spending quality time providing emotional support celebrating achievements and supporting personal growth are essential elements of nurturing relationships. Remember that relationships require investment care and effort from all parties involved. By prioritizing relationship-building skills you can cultivate meaningful and fulfilling connections in your personal and professional life.

# Chapter 14: Building a Supportive Network

Introduction:

In today's world building a supportive network is crucial for personal and professional development. A supportive network consists of individuals who provide emotional support guidance and valuable connections. Having a strong network can help us face challenges explore new opportunities and navigate through various aspects of life. In this chapter we will delve deeper into the importance of building a supportive network and provide examples of how it can positively impact our lives.

1. The Importance of a Supportive Network:

Having a supportive network offers numerous benefits. Let's explore some key reasons why building a supportive network is essential:

a. Emotional Support:

Life can be challenging and having a network of individuals who genuinely care about our well-being can make a significant difference. They can provide a listening ear offer advice and help us navigate through difficult times. Whether it's a personal setback or a professional challenge having emotional support can improve our resilience and overall mental well-being.

b. Access to Different Perspectives:

A supportive network usually consists of people from diverse backgrounds and experiences. This diversity allows us to gain different perspectives on various aspects of life. These alternative viewpoints can broaden our horizons enhance our problem-solving skills and encourage personal growth.

c. Mentorship and Guidance:

Building a supportive network gives us access to mentors and experienced individuals who can guide us through our personal and professional journey. They can offer valuable insights based on their own experiences helping us avoid common pitfalls and make better-informed decisions.

d. Collaboration and Opportunities:

A supportive network often consists of individuals with complementary skills and expertise. These connections can lead to collaborative projects partnerships and opportunities that may not have been accessible otherwise. Building a network of individuals who can support and empower each other can create a positive environment for growth and success.

Examples of Building a Supportive Network:

Now let's explore some examples of how building a supportive network can positively impact different areas of our lives:

1. Professional Growth:

Jane a recent college graduate understands the importance

of building a supportive network for her professional development. She actively attends industry conferences networking events and engages in online communities relevant to her field. Through these connections she has gained access to job openings industry insights mentorship and support. Jane's network helped her secure an internship with a prestigious company that eventually led to a full-time job offer.

2. Entrepreneurship:

John aspires to start his own business but lacks the necessary skills and knowledge. Through networking events and local business communities he connects with experienced entrepreneurs who offer guidance advice and potential partnerships. With their support John gains access to resources industry knowledge and a network of potential clients. This supportive network proves instrumental in helping John launch his successful startup.

3. Personal Development:

Sara is going through a difficult breakup and needs emotional support. She reaches out to friends family and joins a support group where she finds others going through similar experiences. Through these connections Sara receives empathy understanding and resources for healing. Her supportive network guides her towards self-reflection self-care practices and helps her regain her confidence and sense of self.

4. Academic Pursuits:

David a high school student aspires to attend a prestigious university. Recognizing the value of a supportive network he connects with academic advisors teachers and mentors who guide him through the application process. His network provides him with valuable insights essay feedback and interview preparation. With their support David gets accepted into his dream college and achieves his academic goals.

5. Health and Wellness:

Emily is determined to improve her overall health and well-being. She builds a supportive network by joining a gym attending fitness classes and connecting with like-minded individuals. Through these connections Emily gains support motivation and accountability. Her network shares healthy living tips workout routines and provides encouragement during challenging times. With their support Emily achieves her health and wellness goals.

Conclusion:

Building a supportive network is essential for personal and professional growth. It provides emotional support access to different perspectives mentorship collaboration and opportunities. Whether it's in the realm of professional growth entrepreneurship personal development academic pursuits or health and wellness a strong support network can positively impact our lives. By actively seeking connections engaging in networking activities and nurturing relationships we can create a network that empowers and supports us throughout various aspects of life. So invest in building a supportive network as it will serve as a foundation for our success and happiness.

# Chapter 15: Finding Joy in Community

Introduction:

As human beings we are inherently social creatures. We thrive on connection interaction and a sense of belonging. Our sense of community is essential for our overall well-being and can significantly impact our levels of joy and happiness. In this chapter we will explore the concept of finding joy in community delve into its importance and illustrate its impact on our lives through various examples.

What is Community?

Community refers to a group of individuals who share common interests values or geographical proximity. It can take many forms such as a neighborhood workplace school religious group or even an online community. At its core a community provides a sense of belonging support and collective identity.

Importance of Community:

1. Support and Belonging:

Community offers a support system that helps us navigate life's challenges and celebrate its triumphs. It provides a sense of belonging creating a safe space where we can share our joys and concerns. Being part of a community instills a feeling of being seen valued and understood which contributes to our overall happiness.

For example consider a neighborhood community where neighbors regularly organize events like block parties or neighborhood clean-ups. These activities not only foster a sense of togetherness but also offer support during challenging times such as helping each other with home repairs or providing emotional support.

2. Shared Values and Interests:
Communities often gather individuals who share common values goals or interests allowing for a deeper level of connection. Whether it's a sports team book club or volunteer organization being part of a community with shared interests provides a sense of purpose and fulfillment.

Take for instance a group of individuals passionate about environmental conservation forming an eco-conscious community. They come together to collaborate on initiatives like beach clean-ups tree planting and awareness campaigns. This shared purpose not only strengthens their bond but also brings them joy through making a positive impact on the world.

3. Learning and Growth:
Communities can be a rich source of knowledge and wisdom. They facilitate learning and personal growth by offering opportunities for mentorship skill-sharing and constructive feedback. Being part of a community provides an environment conducive

to learning from others' experiences and expertise.

Consider a writing community where aspiring writers gather to share their work offer feedback and exchange writing tips. Through this community individuals can improve their writing skills gain confidence and ultimately find joy in their creative expression.

4. Emotional Well-being:

Community plays a vital role in supporting our emotional well-being. It offers a network of people who can provide emotional support empathy and understanding during challenging times. Sharing our joys and concerns with others helps validate our experiences and provides a safe outlet for emotional expression.

For instance a support group for individuals dealing with loss or grief provides a community where members can openly share their feelings find solace in shared experiences and receive comfort and encouragement.

5. Increased Social Connection:

Humans are social creatures and forging social connections is essential for our overall happiness. Being part of a community allows us to establish and maintain meaningful relationships reducing feelings of isolation and loneliness. Social connection contributes to our overall well-being and helps us find joy in shared experiences.

For example joining a local sports team provides an opportunity to connect with like-minded individuals spend time together and enjoy the thrill of competition. The camaraderie and shared experiences on the field can create lifelong friendships and bring immense joy.

Impact of Community on Joy:

1. Sense of Purpose and Fulfillment:
Being part of a community allows us to find meaning and purpose in our lives. The shared interests values and goals within a community provide a sense of direction and fulfillment. When we actively contribute and participate in a community we experience a deeper level of joy derived from serving a greater purpose.

For instance imagine being involved in a community project to build a playground in a low-income neighborhood. As the project progresses and you see the joy on children's faces when they finally have a safe and fun place to play your sense of purpose and fulfillment will bring immense joy.

2. Increased Positive Emotions:
Being part of a community often entails engaging in activities that bring us joy. These activities may involve shared hobbies celebrations or even volunteering. Engaging in such activities within a community setting amplifies the positive emotions we experience. The collective joy and enthusiasm create an uplifting atmosphere that enhances our individual happiness.

For example attending a music festival surrounded by fellow music lovers creates a ripple effect of joy. The collective energy shared appreciation for music and the spirit of celebration contribute to an overall heightened sense of joy and happiness.

3. Supportive Relationships:

Community fosters supportive relationships that nurture our well-being. Strong social connections built within a community provide a network of emotional support encouragement and love. Knowing that we have people to lean on during tough times and to share our joys with enhances our sense of joy and belonging.

Imagine a new mother joining a parenting support group. Within this community she finds understanding advice and friendship. The shared experiences and support received not only alleviate the challenges of motherhood but also amplify the joy she experiences in the journey of raising her child.

4. Opportunities for Shared Growth:

Communities offer opportunities for personal and collective growth. Through the interactions within a community we learn from others gain new perspectives and expand our horizons. This continuous growth and learning journey contribute to our fulfillment and joy.

Consider a community-based learning program where individuals come together to learn new skills or pursue educational interests. The collaborative nature of the community fosters a positive learning environment allowing for personal growth and the joy of acquiring new knowledge.

Conclusion:

Finding joy in community is a fundamental aspect of our human experience. Through support shared values learning emotional well-being and increased social connection community significantly impacts our levels of happiness and fulfillment. Whether it is the support received during challenging times the joy derived from shared activities and celebrations or the sense of purpose found within a community the impact on our overall well-being is profound. By actively participating in and nurturing our communities we can cultivate deeper connections amplify joy and ultimately lead happier lives.

9 788119 786930

Printed at Repro India Ltd.